MASTERCLASS
Q & A Study Guide for Police Exams

Crime

Series 1 Edition 2

MASTERCLASS
Q & A Study Guide for Police Exams

PASS
MASTERCLASS
Questions

Crime

Series 1 Edition 2

Written by
Fraser Sampson and Glenn Hutton

D_t Detail
Technologies
Limited

Published by
Detail Technologies Limited

Masterclass Pass Questions - Q&A Study Guide for Police Exams
CRIME - Series 1 Edition 2
Fraser Sampson and Glenn Hutton

Detail Technologies Limited
PO Box 43, Porth, CF39 8WR.

British Library Cataloguing in Publication Data
Data available

ISBN 0-9546129-1-4

Designed and typeset by **Splash Design**,
Bridgefield House, Bedwas, Caerphilly, CF83 8DZ
Printed in Great Britain by **MWL Print Group Ltd**,
New Inn, Pontypool, NP4 0DQ

MASTERCLASS
Q & A Study Guide for Police Exams

Contents

Detail Technologies Ltd

Detail Technologies Limited has provided technology based learning aids for police officers for several years. Founded by serving police officers who understand entirely the learning process for the National Police Examinations, the company is dedicated to providing exciting new ways to make studying easier. In addition to the IT products PASS, Quick Questions and Masterclass Questions, the new Masterclass Audio is available on CD for use in the car or away from your computer.

The award winning PASS Part 1 Question Generation Engine is now available to use via the Detail web site. PASS ONLINE™ provides several features found in PASS via a web server. Log on via the website at www.detail-technologies.co.uk and sign up for a free trial. Take an on-line examination. Access a trainer who will be able to answer your legal query or partake in discussions via the on-line legal bulletin board.

Quick Questions Mobile allows you to receive questions by textphone. Text EXAM to 88199 and you will be sent a question by return. Send your answer and you will be told whether you are correct or wrong.

All Detail products are designed to enhance your chances of exam success. For further information telephone 0870 800 2 999 or check out www.detail-technologies.co.uk.

The Authors

Fraser Sampson LL.B., LL.M., MBA Solicitor

Formerly the Head of National Police Training Examinations & Assessment, Fraser Sampson has considerable experience in the strategic and operational management of assessment, selection, recruitment processes and professional qualifying examinations. While working for the Home Office, Fraser provided advice to the Police Promotion Examinations Board and several advisory groups. Having published many articles across a range of professional journals, Fraser is the author of several current professional texts including the best-selling Blackstone's Police Manuals (published by Oxford University Press). Fraser is now a qualified solicitor practising at the award winning national law firm, Walker Morris, where he specialises in Employment and Police work.

Glenn Hutton BA., M.Phil., FCIPD

Glenn Hutton is co-author of the Blackstone Police Manual Evidence and Procedure. He was formerly Head of Examinations and Assessment and Quality Assurance for National Police Training (now Centrex), Head of Training in North Yorkshire Police and worked as a Course Director and Director of Studies at the Police Staff College, Bramshill.

Glenn currently works as a private consultant to organisations concerned with recruitment and selection by way of assessment and examination and is the author of three educational text books on key skills examinations.

SERGEANTS

Crime

Question CR/PS/1

Some offences are classified as crimes of **'basic intent'**.

Which of the following statements is true in relation to such offences?

A They must be 'complete' offences and can not be 'attempted'.

B They can not be committed by 'recklessness'.

C They do not require proof of any particular or 'ulterior' intention.

D They are triable summarily.

Answer CR/PS/1

C is correct.

By definition, these offences only require proof of a basic intention. These offences can be 'attempted' like most other offences and recklessness will suffice. The mode of trial is irrelevant.

Question CR/PS/2

You have charged someone with an offence of criminal damage after they threw a lighted cigarette-end into a litter bin causing the bin to catch fire.

In proving the defendant's mens rea or state of mind at the time, what provision does *R v G and R* [2003] 3 WLR 1060 make?

A   R v G and R [2003] 3 WLR 1060 is no longer used to establish 'recklessness' - the test is now based on objective 'Caldwell Recklessness'.

B   A person will be 'reckless' as to circumstances when s/he is aware of the risk that existed or would exist.

C   A person will be 'reckless' as to circumstances when s/he is not aware of the risk that existed and in the circumstances known to him/her, unreasonable to take the risk.

D   A person will be 'reckless' as to circumstances when s/he is aware of the risk that existed or would exist and in the circumstances known to him/her, unreasonable to take the risk.

Answer CR/PS/2

D is correct.

In establishing 'recklessness' in Criminal Damage cases - the old objective 'Caldwell test' has now been replaced by a subjective test highlighted in *R v G and R* **[2003] 3 WLR 1060**. Their Lordships held that a person acts recklessly for the purposes of criminal damage on the following basis: a person will be 'reckless' as to circumstances when s/he is aware of a risk that existed or would exist, and it is, in the circumstances known to him/her, unreasonable to take the risk.

Question CR/PS/3

Some offences require proof of objective recklessness.

In relation to objective recklessness (in particular 'Caldwell Recklessness'), which of the following is INCORRECT?

A   It will not apply where the defendant was unable to see the risk themselves.

B   It will apply where the defendant fails to consider an obvious risk.

C   It will apply where the defendant 'turns a blind eye' to an obvious risk.

D   It will not apply to occasions where the defendant has actually recognised the risk but gone ahead with their actions.

Answer CR/PS/3

A is correct.

Objective recklessness does not take account of whether the defendant could foresee the risk or not - however unfair or harsh that may be!

Question CR/PS/4

During a fight in a taxi queue, Laitner picks up a litter bin and throws it at Bernard intending to injure him. The bin misses Bernard but hits a bystander, bouncing off him and breaking a shop window.

In relation to the 'doctrine of transferred malice', which of the following statements is true?

A   The doctrine would apply equally to any injury sustained by the bystander and to the damage caused to the shop window.

B   The doctrine would not apply to any injury sustained by the bystander or to the damage caused to the shop window.

C   The doctrine would apply to the damage caused to the shop window.

D   The doctrine would apply to any injury sustained by the bystander.

Answer CR/PS/4

D is correct.

The doctrine can only transfer the relevant mens rea or state of mind from one intended offence to a similar offence. As the intended offence was an assault, the doctrine will apply to any further assault but not to an offence of criminal damage.

Question CR/PS/5

'Mens rea' is what a defendant must have had, 'actus reus' is what a defendant must have done or failed to do.

In which of the following instances might the 'omission' be enough to amount to the 'actus reus' or criminal conduct?

A   Burke, a do-it-yourself enthusiast, fits a gas fire in a friend's home. Burke forgets to line the chimney flue and the friend becomes seriously ill as a result of carbon monoxide poisoning.

B   Llewelyn, a retired police officer, witnesses a person being seriously assaulted in the street. Llewelyn does not intervene and the victim of the assault dies as a result of her injuries.

C   Martin, an 18 year old, sees his neighbour's 14 year son about to break into a car. Martin does not stop the boy who breaks the car window and steals a coat from the vehicle.

D   Siddiqi, a chemistry teacher, accidentally sets fire to a bench in the school chemistry laboratory. He moves to an adjacent classroom to finish the experiment he is conducting before trying to tackle the fire which subsequently spreads to an adjacent classroom.

Answer CR/PS/5

D is correct.

Creating a situation of danger and then failing to counteract that danger is an occasion where an omission may amount to actus reus or criminal conduct. The relationship between the 'offender' and the victim is important in omission cases and must be one which would attract a 'duty' to act. A retired police officer is no longer under a legal duty to act, neither is someone who is not in a parental or other 'duty' relationship with a child.

Question CR/PS/6

Kamal has been arrested after breaking into the house of an old age pensioner and steals a television. The occupier, a 79 year old man who is in poor health, is very distressed by the incident and by the subsequent police attendance. As a result of this distress, the pensioner's illness is aggravated and he dies two days later.

The investigating officer wants to charge Kamal with manslaughter.

What is Kamal's criminal liability, if any, in relation to the pensioner's death?

A Kamal may have committed manslaughter as there is a 'causal link' between the burglary and the death.

B Kamal can not be held responsible for the death which was the result of an existing medical condition.

C Kamal has committed a burglary which is an offence against property, therefore there can not be a 'causal link' with the death of the pensioner.

D Kamal can not be held responsible for the death unless he knew of the pensioner's medical condition and nevertheless went on to commit the burglary.

Answer CR/PS/6

A is correct.

There is a causal link between the burglary and the death, even if it only aggravates an existing medical condition. The common law recognises a causal link in such cases and the nature of the offence is irrelevant. In these cases a defendant must **'take their victim as they find them'** and there is no requirement for them to have any knowledge about their victim's state of health.

Question CR/PS/7

A drug dealer has been arrested after being seen selling a wrap of heroin to a 16 year old girl. The girl, who was not apprehended, subsequently took the heroin which had been 'cut' with rat poison by the drug dealer. She is admitted to hospital who inform you, the investigating officer, that she has lapsed into a coma.

What, if any, is the 'causal link' between the drug dealer's conduct and the girl's injuries?

A His conduct was the direct cause of the injuries so there is a causal link.

B His conduct was not the direct cause of the girl's injuries as the girl exercised her own free will in taking the drug, therefore there is no causal link.

C His conduct was reckless in supplying her with a dangerous mix of heroin and poison, therefore there is a causal link.

D His conduct was the indirect cause of the injuries and, because the girl was a minor, there is a causal link.

Answer CR/PS/7

B is correct.

The girl's deliberate exercise of free will breaks any causal link that there may have been. The conduct was not the direct cause of the injuries.

Recklessness is an issue of mens rea or state of mind; it is irrelevant to causation, as is the girl's age.

Question CR/PS/8

You are investigating a stabbing outside a night club. The victim is escorted in the ambulance to hospital where he is treated by a doctor. The doctor correctly treats the victim with a painkilling drug but the victim has a severe allergic reaction to the treatment and dies as a result.

In relation to the victim's death, which of the following statements is true?

A The medical treatment was the direct cause of death. Therefore the person who stabbed the victim can only be held responsible for the stabbing and not the death.

B The doctor who treated the patient owed them a 'duty of care' in prescribing any medication and is therefore solely responsible for the victim's death.

C The medical treatment was correctly prescribed and therefore no-one has any criminal liability for the victim's death.

D The medical treatment was a natural consequence of the stabbing and, as it was correctly prescribed, the person who stabbed the victim is responsible for the death.

Answer CR/PS/8

D is correct.

Medical treatment, properly given, will not normally be regarded as an **'intervening act'** which breaks the **'causal link'**. The doctor's duty of care is irrelevant in this case. Had the treatment been given negligently, the doctor may have attracted some criminal liability.

Question CR/PS/9

Morton, a 17 year old working at an off-licence, tells his colleague Jefferies to 'help himself' to some bottles of wine in the shop storeroom. Morton has been told by the manager that employees must not take any goods without seeking permission first. Jefferies takes no notice of Morton and leaves the wine where it is.

In relation to 'incomplete' offences, which of the following statements is true?

A   Morton and Jefferies commit the offence of conspiracy.

B   Morton commits the offence of incitement.

C   Morton commits the offence of attempted theft.

D   Morton and Jefferies commit the offence of attempted theft.

Answer CR/PS/9

B is correct.

The offence of incitement involves the encouraging of another to commit an offence. The other person need not go on to commit that offence. Morton has not carried out any acts which are 'more than merely preparatory' to the commission of the theft. It is not a 'conspiracy' as there was never an 'agreement' between Morton and Jefferies.

Question CR/PS/10

Vernon and Michael Edwards are doormen at a night club. In order to get a doorman from a rival firm arrested, Vernon and Michael agree to stage an assault. Vernon allows Michael to punch him in the face causing a black eye and fracturing his cheek. Both doormen then report the incident to the police saying that it was the doorman from the rival firm who was responsible for the assault.

In relation to 'conspiracy', which of the following statements is true?

A There is no statutory conspiracy because the only co-conspirator (Vernon) was also the intended victim.

B There is no statutory conspiracy because perverting the course of justice is a common law offence.

C There is a common law conspiracy because a person can not consent to such a serious assault.

D There is a statutory conspiracy because two people have agreed on a course of conduct which will amount to the commission of an offence by them.

Answer CR/PS/10

D is correct.

Vernon and Michael have agreed on a course of action which, if carried out in accordance with their intentions, would amount to the commission of an offence (perverting the course of justice) by one or both of them.

Vernon is not the 'intended victim' of the conspiracy; he is the victim of the assault. The course of justice is the intended 'victim' here. The source of the intended offence is irrelevant and common law conspiracies are those which are intended to defraud.

Question CR/PS/11

Rodber is in prison on remand for drug trafficking offences. Rodber is visited in prison by his wife Marlene and a family friend called Butcher. The three of them agree on a plan to help Rodber escape from the prison. Before they can implement the plan, Rodber is transferred to another prison.

Who, if anyone, commits an offence of statutory conspiracy?

A   Marlene and Butcher.

B   Marlene, Butcher and Rodber.

C   Rodber and Butcher.

D   No one.

Answer CR/PS/11

B is correct.

All three have agreed on a course of action which, if carried out in accordance with their intentions, would amount to the commission of an offence (escaping/assisting escape) by one or all of them. Ordinarily spouses can not 'conspire' with each other. However, a spouse can be guilty of conspiracy if the agreement also involves a third party.

A statutory conspiracy was committed at the time the agreement was made. The fact that it was frustrated by circumstances at the last minute is irrelevant.

Question CR/PS/12

Harrison goes to a party at a friend's house one night. Although Harrison says he is not going to drink too much, some people at the party think it would be a 'laugh' to spike his drinks with spirits. After a while, Harrison begins to feel unwell and decides to walk home. He passes a newsagent's and, because he is now very drunk, decides he would like a newspaper. Not thinking that the shop might be closed, Harrison tries the door.

Finding it to be locked, Harrison begins to shoulder-barge the door of the shop. He is seen by a police patrol and is arrested for attempted burglary under section **9(1)(a) of the Theft Act 1968.**

On these facts, does Harrison appear to have a defence to the charge?

A   No, he carried out acts which were more than merely preparatory to the offence and therefore commits an attempted burglary under s. 9(1)(a).

B   Yes, because he mistakenly thought that the shop was open.

C   No, because drunkenness is not a defence to burglary.

D   Yes, burglary under s. 9(1)(a) is a crime of specific intent and Harrison's drunkenness was 'involuntary'.

Answer CR/PS/12

D is correct.

Harrison's intoxication was involuntary, therefore he could not form the required intent to commit a crime of specific intent - such as burglary under s. 9(1)(a). Harrison's initial 'mistake' is irrelevant. If he had mistakenly thought that the shop was open and simply tried to get into the shop, he may have had a defence of 'mistake'. If Harrison had knowingly got himself drunk, then he would not have been able to claim this as a defence.

Question CR/PS/13

A physical and self defence trainer at a police training centre is showing off to her students after a class. Claiming that she can aim a round-house kick over the top of the open door of a probationer's car, she takes a kick. As she had overestimated her kicking prowess, the woman does not reach high enough and breaks the car window.

Which of the following statements is true in relation to a possible defence of 'mistake'?

A   If the trainer reasonably believed that she could demonstrate the kick without damaging the window, she has a defence of 'mistake'.

B   If the trainer gave no thought to the possibility of the window breaking, she has no defence of 'mistake'.

C   If the trainer did all that she could reasonably do to miss the window, she has a defence of 'mistake'.

D   If the trainer held an honest belief that she could demonstrate the kick without damaging the window, she has a defence of 'mistake'.

Answer CR/PS/13

B is correct.

Inadvertence (i.e. mistakes) in crimes of basic intent - such as criminal damage - will not amount to a defence. Reasonable belief in her own ability does not amount to a defence of 'mistake', neither does taking all reasonable care but still going on to carry out the act. An honestly held belief in her own ability does not amount to a defence of 'mistake' either.

See *Chief Constable of Avon and Somerset Police v Shimmen* **(1986) 84 Cr App R 7**

Question CR/PS/14

Believing that he is about to be attacked with a knife, an under cover police officer strikes a football supporter with a telescopic metal truncheon. The football supporter is knocked unconscious and suffers a severe laceration to his eye. Later enquiries reveal that the supporter did not have a knife and that the officer had not been in any danger.

In relation to the officer's claim of 'self-defence', which of the following statements is true?

A The officer was not entitled to 'strike the first blow' under the circumstances.

B The officer's claim will be a question of law for the magistrate/judge to decide.

C The officer's use of force will be assessed against the circumstances as he honestly believed them to be.

D The officer must show that he made all reasonable efforts to retreat from the anticipated attack before defending himself.

Answer CR/PS/14

C is correct.

That is the basis for determining the reasonableness or otherwise of a defendant's conduct in self-defence. There is no requirement to let an attacker/believed attacker strike the first blow. The question of whether a defendant acted in self-defence or not is a question of fact. There is no requirement to retreat from an attacker/believed attacker.

Question CR/PS/15

During a domestic dispute, a woman in her 28th week of pregnancy is attacked by her former boyfriend. Knowing that she is pregnant, the boyfriend kicks the woman in the abdomen causing her to have a miscarriage. The officers attending the incident want to charge the boyfriend with murder.

In relation to the offence of murder, what is the boyfriend's criminal liability?

A If the foetus was capable of being born alive, it would be 'another human being' for the purposes of the offence of murder as 'malice' can be transferred .

B As the boyfriend intended to injure the woman, he can not be held responsible for injuries to the unborn child.

C As the miscarriage occurred within a year and a day of the assault, the boyfriend may be guilty of an offence of murder.

D As the child was not born alive, it can not be 'another human being' for the purpose of the offence of murder.

Answer CR/PS/15

D is correct.

The expression 'another human being' does not extend to unborn children however far advanced in their development. The capability of a child being born alive is irrelevant to the offence of murder (it is relevant to the offence of child destruction). The doctrine of transferred malice is irrelevant unless the child is born alive, while the 'year and a day' rule has been removed.

Question CR/PS/16

In relation to the offence of manslaughter by an 'unlawful act', which of the following statements is true?

A   The act can be directed towards property as well as another person.

B   The act must be directed at a person.

C   The act can include an omission.

D   The act must be intended or likely to cause harm.

Answer CR/PS/16

A is correct.

The courts have decided that unlawful acts towards property which bring about the death of another can amount to manslaughter and the acts are not limited to those directed at people. Omissions are not included and there is no requirement for an intention/likelihood of harm.

Question CR/PS/17

Dillon, a 23 year old student, is arrested for shoplifting. When he is searched in your custody area, a quantity of LSD tablets are found in the pocket of the jacket he is wearing. When questioned, Dillon states that he has borrowed the jacket from a friend.

In bringing a charge of 'possession' of the controlled drug against Dillon, the officer in the case would have to prove that Dillon knew:

A   That the tablets were in the jacket and that they were LSD.

B   That the tablets were in the jacket and that they were a controlled drug.

C   That the tablets were a controlled drug.

D   That the tablets were in the jacket.

Answer CR/PS/17

D is correct.

He must know of the presence of the tablets which are in fact a controlled drug. Knowledge of the quality of something is not necessary in order to be in 'possession' of it for these purposes.

Question CR/PS/18

Section 28 of the Misuse of Drugs Act 1971 provides a general defence to certain offences under the Act.

Which of the following is NOT covered by this general defence?

A   Unlawful possession of a controlled drug.

B   Possession with intent to supply a controlled drug.

C   Conspiracy to supply a controlled drug.

D   The unlawful cultivation of cannabis.

Answer CR/PS/18

C is correct.

Conspiracies are offences at common law and are not covered by the s.28 general defence under the Act.

Question CR/PS/19

The Headteacher at a High School finds a pupil to be in possession of a 'Dollar' ecstasy tablet which is a controlled drug. Believing it to be a controlled drug, the Headteacher confiscates it and flushes it down the lavatory to prevent the pupil from committing any further offence in relation to the tablet. She then telephones your police station to say what she has done.

In relation to the offence of unlawful possession of a controlled drug under the Misuse of Drugs Act 1971, which of the following statements is true?

A   The Headteacher has a statutory defence.

B   The Headteacher does not have a statutory defence because she did not take all steps reasonably open to her to deliver the drug to a person lawfully entitled to possess it.

C   The Headteacher has a defence at common law.

D   The Headteacher does not have a statutory defence because she knew or believed the tablet to be a controlled drug.

Answer CR/PS/19

A is correct.

The defence under s. 5(4) Misuse of Drugs Act 1971 fits the circumstances. The defence under s.5(4) specifically allows for destruction of the drug. There is no such defence at common law and the defence under s. 5(4) applies to people knowing or believing something to be a controlled drug.

Question CR/PS/20

Bradley is stopped after being observed by a constable to drive his vehicle through a red traffic light. He is then arrested after providing a positive breath test and taken to the police station. As custody officer you receive Bradley and during a search he is found to be in possession of a quantity of cannabis. When interviewed about being in possession of cannabis Bradley states that the previous evening he had found the substance in his 16 year old son's bedroom and taken possession of it intending to hand it in at the local surgery, on his return from work today.

In these circumstances would Bradley have a statutory defence under s.5(4) for his possession of a controlled drug?

A   Yes, if he can prove that whilst the controlled drug was in his possession he had no intention of using or supplying the drug for his or another's use.

B   No, as soon as possible after taking possession on the controlled drug he must have taken steps for its immediate destruction.

C   Yes, he was preventing another from committing or continuing to commit an offence and intended to deliver it into the custody of a medical practitioner as soon as he possibly could.

D   No, he must have taken all reasonable steps to deliver the controlled drug to a police officer or HM Customs & Excise officer and not a medical practitioner.

Answer CR/PS/20

Answer C is correct.

The Misuse of Drugs Act 1971 s. 5(4) provides a defence where a person takes possession of a controlled drug to prevent another from committing or continuing to commit an offence in connection with that drug. This is provided that they take all reasonable steps to destroy the drug or take it to someone lawfully entitled to possess it as soon as possible after taking possession of it. A person 'lawfully entitled to possess it' would include a police officer or an officer of HM Customs and Excise **AND** a medical practitioner.

Question CR/PS/21

You are a section sergeant when one of your community constable's seeks your advice. The constable informs you that she is dealing with several complaints from residents of young people 'glue sniffing' in a local park and believes the substances used are being obtained from a local hardware shop. She has also ascertained that the young people are using butane lighter fuel as an intoxicant and she is unsure of the law in this area.

In relation to the advice that you would give the constable which one of the following statements is correct?

A   It is an offence for a person to supply a butane lighter refill to a person under 18 if that person knows them to be under that age.

B   It is an offence to supply any cigarette lighter refill canister containing butane to any person under 18.

C   It is an offence for a person to supply a butane lighter refill to a person under 16 if that person has reasonable cause to suspect them to be under that age.

D   It is an offence to supply any cigarette lighter refill canister containing butane to any person under 16.

Answer CR/PS/21

B is correct.

The Cigarette Lighter Refill (Safety) Regulations 1999 (SI 1999/1844) provide that no person shall supply any cigarette lighter refill canister containing butane or a substance with butane as a constituent part to any person under the age of eighteen. There is no requirement to show that person knew or suspect them to be under 18.

Question CR/PS/22

Logdon wants to frighten his next door neighbour with whom he has had a running feud for several months. Logdon takes a toy pistol from his son's bedroom and goes round to the neighbour's house. Logdon points the toy pistol at the neighbour and shouts "Say your prayers, I'm going to finish you off once and for all." The neighbour believes that the pistol is real and that Logdon will shoot him. After a few seconds Logdon laughs and walks away. The neighbour calls the police.

Does Logdon's conduct amount to an 'assault'?

A   No, because there has been no immediate application of unlawful force.

B   Yes, because Logdon has caused the neighbour anxiety which amounts to the immediate use of unlawful force.

C   No, because words alone can not amount to an assault.

D   Yes, because the neighbour believed that the pistol was real and apprehended the immediate use of unlawful force.

Answer CR/PS/22

D is correct.

Causing the apprehension of immediate unlawful force under these circumstances will amount to an assault. The anxiety caused is not the immediate use of unlawful force and words can amount to an assault, although in this case they are also accompanied by actions (pointing the pistol).

Question CR/PS/23

After a neighbour complains to police about Eire's anti-social behaviour, Eire begins to make menacing telephone calls to the neighbour's wife. The neighbour's wife is a very nervous character and the nature of the calls has such an effect on her that she suffers severe mental trauma requiring long-term psychiatric treatment.

Can Eire be charged with an offence under section 20 of the Offences Against the Person Act 1861?

A   No, because he has not 'wounded' the wife or 'inflicted' any harm.

B   Yes, because Eire must 'take his victim as he finds her' and therefore provided he has foreseen the consequences of his actions, he will be guilty of the offence.

C   Yes, because his actions have indirectly 'inflicted' grievous bodily harm and Eire acted 'unlawfully and maliciously'.

D   No, because the injury caused is psychological and therefore can not amount to 'grievous bodily harm'.

Answer CR/PS/23

C is correct.

Grievous bodily harm - which can include psychological injury - may be caused indirectly and Eire acts both 'maliciously and unlawfully' in doing so. Eire has inflicted the harm, albeit indirectly. The rule requiring an assailant to 'take their victim as they find them' and the issue of foresight are not linked. The rule relates to a 'causal link', i.e. the consequences of someone's conduct (which exists in this case) but that does not mean to say that Eire - or anyone else - will be presumed to have foreseen those consequences which is an issue of intent.

Question CR/PS/24

In proving an offence under section 20 of the Offences Against the Person Act 1861, what behaviour will amount to 'maliciously'?

A Foresight by the defendant of the degree of harm which is caused to the victim.

B Some element of premeditation or preparation.

C Ignoring a risk of harm which would have been obvious to any reasonable person at the time.

D Ignoring a risk of harm which was apparent to the defendant at the time.

Answer CR/PS/24

D is correct.

The expression 'maliciously' means acting with subjective recklessness. There is no need for the defendant to foresee the degree of harm which is eventually brought about by their actions; only that some harm may be brought about. The offence requires subjective recklessness not objective recklessness.

Question CR/PS/25

During an under 21's rugby match, the scrum-half from the home team, is tackled forcefully by Dennis, a forward on the opposing team. The scrum-half who was running with the ball, is brought to the ground causing him to be heavily concussed and fracturing his neck. A spectator feels that Dennis should be sent off and shouts abuse at him and the referee.

Dennis hears him and the next time Dennis is on that side of the field, he runs into touch, hoping to hit the spectator but collides with someone else instead, breaking their nose. An off duty police officer is at the game and arrests Dennis after the match.

On the facts set out, does Dennis incur any criminal liability in relation to the injuries which he has caused?

A   No, both injuries - though serious - were caused during a properly-conducted sporting event.

B   Yes, but only in relation to the injured spectator as the scrum-half had 'consented' to any injuries caused during the ordinary course of the game.

C   Yes in respect of both injuries as the scrum-half can not 'consent' to a broken neck and the incident involving the spectator was outside the parameters of the game.

D   No, because the scrum-half had 'consented' to any injuries caused during the ordinary course of the game and the injury to the spectator was not caused intentionally.

Answer CR/PS/25

B is correct.

The scrum-half can 'consent', even to serious harm caused during the ordinary course of a properly-conducted sporting event. The injury to the spectator went beyond proper participation in the sporting event and some injury to the spectator could have been foreseen by Dennis because his intention to injure the first spectator was transferred to the second.

Question CR/PS/26

While investigating an allegation of incivility to a member of the public, a civilian personnel manager in your police station finds two members of staff who are suspected of the alleged behaviour in the staff changing room, getting ready to go home. Telling them to "stay put", he locks the door to the locker room and goes to make further enquiries among his supervisors. The staff remain locked in the room for five minutes before the manager returns and allows them to leave the shop. The staff members call you.

Does the manager commit an offence of false imprisonment?

A   Yes, because he has unlawfully restrained the free movement of his staff.

B   No, because he has not actually 'imprisoned' the members of staff, he has merely impeded their ability to leave for a short time.

C   No, because there must be a degree of 'removal' or 'taking' of the victim to some other place.

D   Yes, because he has acted in a way which would be seen as 'unreasonable' by an objective bystander.

Answer CR/PS/26

A is correct.

The ingredients of the offence are the unlawful and intentional/reckless restraint of a person's freedom of movement for however short a period. Thus because the personnel manager has no 'legal authority' to restrain the movement of his staff (by locking them in a room) he has technically committed the offence of false imprisonment. There is no requirement for any "taking or removal" as there is in the offence of kidnapping and objective reasonableness is not relevant for this offence.

Question CR/PS/27

In relation to the offence of torture under section 134 of the Criminal Justice Act 1988, which of the following statements is correct?

A   It can only be committed by a 'public official'.

B   It can only be committed if the person is acting within the United Kingdom.

C   It includes the infliction of mental suffering.

D   It can not be committed by an omission.

Answer CR/PS/27

C is correct.

Subsection (3) includes mental suffering within the ambit of the offence. It can be committed by others provided they are acting in conjunction with a public official or person acting in an official capacity and it can be committed 'in the UK or elsewhere' **(see subs. 1 and 2(a))**. Subsection (3) includes omissions within the ambit of the offence.

Question CR/PS/28

Williams who is separated from his wife offers her £200 to have sexual intercourse with him. Initially she refuses but, after he continues to pester her, she reluctantly agrees. Williams has no intention of paying her the money. After they have begun to have sexual intercourse, Williams' wife changes her mind and tells Williams to stop. Williams says that they have an 'agreement' and continues until the point of ejaculation.

Does Williams commit the offence of rape contrary to s.1 of the Sexual Offences Act 2003?

A   No, because his wife consented to having sexual intercourse with him, even though he had no intention of paying her the agreed sum.

B   No, because, although separated, Williams was still lawfully married to his wife and there can be no offence of rape in such circumstances.

C   Yes, because the wife's consent was obtained by fraud, which is specifically mentioned in s.75 as an 'act' which negates any 'consent' which can be given.

D   Yes, because, although she gives her consent at the outset, Williams' wife withdraws that consent during sexual intercourse.

Answer CR/PS/28

D is correct.

Consent, once given, can be withdrawn at any time. Although initially valid, his wife's consent is later withdrawn. The consent to the act of sexual intercourse was given freely, even though Williams did not intend to pay. The nature of the proposed act was never in doubt. A man can commit the offence against his wife, even if they are still co-habiting.

Note
Fraud is not an 'open' act covered by s.75 Evidential Presumption & Consent.

***R v Cooper* [1994] Crim LR 531 -**
Once the 'passive' party to sexual penetration withdraws consent, any continued activity (e.g. penetration) can amount to a sexual offence [i.e. rape].

Question CR/PS/29

Johnson attends a snooker club with some cards advertising the services of a local prostitute he knows. He enters the snooker club (which bars entry to people who are under 16 years of age) and pins some of the cards on a notice board above a public phone which members of the snooker club can use to make outgoing calls only.

In relation to s.46 Criminal Justice and Police Act 2001 has Johnson committed an indictable offence?

A   Yes, the offence is complete.

B   No, although the offence is indictable, the snooker club is not a public place as it restricts members to people who are over 16 years of age.

C   No, placing cards in the vicinity of a public telephone is not covered by the act.

D   No, the offence is complete but it isn't an indictable offence.

Answer CR/PS/29

B is correct.

This offence of placing adverts for prostitutes near public phones is an indictable offence.

s.46 of the Criminal Justice and Police Act 2001 states:

(1) A person commits an offence if -
(a) he places on, or in the immediate vicinity of a public telephone, an advertisement relating to prostitution, and
(b) he does so with the intention that the advertisement should come to the attention of any other person or persons.

Section 46(5) gives a very specific definition of 'public place' for the purposes of this offence, namely:

> *any place to which the public have or are permitted to have access (on payment or otherwise), **OTHER THAN***
> - *a place to which children under 16 years of age are not permitted to have access (by law or otherwise), or*
> - *premises used wholly or mainly as residential premises.*

Question CR/PS/30

While playing out in the garden of his parents' house, Garfield, a 13 year old boy, is approached by two youths. The youths persuade Garfield to go with them to an amusement arcade. Even though he does not know the youths and he has been told by his parents not to leave the garden, Garfield goes with the youths quite willingly. The parents ring the police starting a widespread manhunt. After several hours of playing on the machines and rides, the youths leave Garfield in the arcade and he makes his own way home.

Which of the following statements is true in relation to the youths' criminal liability?

A   They commit an offence of kidnapping at common law.

B   They commit no offence as Garfield freely consents to go with them.

C   They commit no offences as they have no parental responsibility for Garfield.

D   They commit an offence of child abduction under s 2 of the Child Abduction Act 1984.

Answer CR/PS/30

D is correct.

The youths take Garfield - a child under 16 - without lawful authority or reasonable excuse, so as to remove him from the lawful control of his parents. The consent of the victim in such circumstances is generally irrelevant, as is the issue of parental responsibility on the part of the youths.

s.2 of the Child Abduction Act 1984 states:

(1) ...a person... if, without lawful authority or reasonable excuse, takes or detains a child under 16 -
  (a) so as to remove him from the lawful control of any person having lawful control of the child, or
  (b) so as to keep him out of the lawful control of any person entitled to lawful control of the child.

Note:
It cannot be kidnapping as Garfield consents and goes along by his own free will.

Child Protection
Child Abduction

Question CR/PS/31

Section 2 of the Theft Act 1968 provides for certain occasions when a person's appropriation of property will not be regarded as dishonest. One such occasion is set out at s. 2(1)(a) and relates to occasions where a person appropriates property in the belief that (s)he has a lawful right to deprive the other of it.

In relation to that belief, which of the following conditions will apply?

A   The belief must be reasonable.

B   The belief must be objective.

C   The belief must be honestly held.

D   The belief must be justified.

Answer CR/PS/31

C is correct.

Such a belief must be honestly held. There is no further
requirement in relation to the belief, other than the belief must
be honestly held.

Question CR/PS/32

Gomez walks into a high street electrical retail store and selects a number of expensive items including stereo music systems and washing machines. He then goes to the sales representative, a friend of his, and says that he wishes to 'pay' for the goods using a stolen cheque. The sales representative, now knowing that the cheque is stolen, agrees to go along with Gomez and endorses the cheque as valid, taking it to the sales manager. The sales manager accepts the cheque as genuine and consents to the release of the goods and authorises them to be loaded into Gomez's van.

Has Gomez 'appropriated' the goods under the requirements of s.3 of the Theft Act 1968?

A   Yes, even though the owner (the sales manager) freely consented to their removal.

B   No, because the owner (the sales manager) freely consented to their removal.

C   No, because Gomez did not actually do anything that could be classed as assuming the rights of the owner.

D   No, because the owner (the sales manager) was acting in good faith and transferred the rights of ownership for value to Gomez.

Answer CR/PS/32

A is correct.

The circumstances outlined are similar to those in *R v Gomez*
[1993] AC 442 where the House of Lords held that such
behaviour amounted to an appropriation. Consent of the owner
is irrelevant to the issue of appropriation. Gomez has assumed
some rights of the owner by receiving the goods into his
possession. The issue of transfer of title (under s. 3(3)) is
irrelevant here.

Question CR/PS/33

A woman was carrying her fifteen month old child and was waiting to cross the road at a pedestrian crossing. A vehicle travelling from her right stopped and she stepped onto the crossing. She then heard a squeal of brakes and saw a car travelling from her left braking heavily and eventually coming to a stop on the crossing itself. The woman shouted an obscenity at the driver who alighted from his vehicle and punched the woman a glancing blow on her shoulder. This caused her to drop the child to the floor where it sustained extensive bruising and lacerations to its legs, left arm and head. The woman received slight bruising to her shoulder.

As custody officer you are considering any charge(s) which may be brought against the driver. In relation to these circumstances are the elements for a charge of assault occasioning actual bodily harm against the driver fulfilled?

A   No, the assault was directed against the woman pedestrian and the driver had no intention of injuring the child.

B   Yes, for the assault on the woman pedestrian who as a result of the driver's application of direct force caused bruising to her shoulder.

C   No, the injury sustained by the woman pedestrian was only slight bruising and insufficient to support a charge of assault occasioning actual bodily harm.

D   Yes, for the assault of the child caused indirectly by punching the woman pedestrian on the shoulder and causing her to drop her child which sustained extensive bruising and lacerations to its legs, left arm and head.

Question CR/PS/33

D is correct.

In *Haystead v Chief Constable of Derbyshire* **[2001] 3 All ER 890** it was held that force can be applied directly or indirectly and that where a defendant punched a woman causing her to drop and injure a child she was holding he was convicted of assaulting that child. See 'Transferred Malice.'

In relation to the woman pedestrian, for 'bruising' to be sufficient to substantiate a charge of assault occasioning actual bodily harm the bruising would need to be 'extensive or multiple' (CPS Charging Standards).

Question CR/PS/34

You are performing the duties of custody officer when one of your constables seeks your advice. She is dealing with the case of a woman who is undergoing medical treatment for a severe psychiatric disorder which it is alleged was caused as a result of a number of menacing telephone calls from her ex-boyfriend.

In considering an offence of inflicting grievous bodily harm under s. 20 of the Offences Against the Person Act 1861 what would your advice be to the constable?

A   No actual assault is necessary and although grievous bodily harm can include psychiatric harm this must be inflicted directly.

B   Even though grievous bodily harm can include psychiatric harm there must be an actual assault upon any other person.

C   No actual assault is necessary and grievous bodily harm, which can include psychiatric harm, can be inflicted indirectly.

D   Grievous bodily harm does not include psychiatric harm for the purpose of this section.

Answer CR/PS/34

C is correct.

The Offences Against the Person Act 1861 provides that whoever shall unlawfully and maliciously wound or inflict grievous bodily harm upon any other person, either with or without any weapon or instrument, shall be guilty of an offence.

In *R v Ireland* **[1998] AC 147** the House of Lords held that no assault is needed for this offence and that harm could be inflicted indirectly, which in this case was inflicting psychiatric harm by menacing telephone calls.

Question CR/PS/35

Armitage (a 17 year old female) has been interviewed in relation to an offence of Sexual Activity with a Child under 16 years (contrary to s.9 of the Sexual Offences Act 2003). During the interview Armitage admitted having penetrative consentual intercourse with a 15 year old boy. Armitage stated that the boy told her he was 16 at the time and that she believed him. You are now considering whether there is sufficient evidence to substantiate a s.9 charge.

Which of the following is true?

A   As the boy was under 16 and Armitage reasonably believed this there is insufficient evidence to charge for a s.9 offence.

B   Armitage commits the s.9 offence as she is over 16 years of age - there is sufficient evidence to charge.

C   If Armitage 'reasonably believed' that the boy was under 16 this will be a defence she can use at trial and should not prevent her from being charged with the s.9 offence.

D   As the boy was under 16 years Armitage's reliance on her holding a reasonable belief that the boy was 16 or over is relevant and she should not be charged with a s.9 offence.

Answer CR/PS/35

D is correct.

Section 9 of the Sexual Offences Act 2003 states:

(1) A person aged 18 or over (A) commits an offence if -
    (a) he intentionally touches another person (B),
    (b) the touching is sexual, and
    (c) either
        (i) B is under 16 and A does not reasonably believe that
            B is 16 or over, or
        (ii) B is under 13.

Thus: As the boy was under 16 and Armitage reasonably believed this there is insufficient evidence to charge for a s.9 offence as neither of the elements of section (c) is satisfied. The 'reasonable belief' element is now part of the 'points to prove' and is no longer a 'legal defence' therefore the option - Reasonable belief of a person being under 16 will be a defence for Armitage and will not prevent her from being charged with a s.9 offence - is incorrect.

Considering the option - Armitage commits the s.9 offence as she is over 16 years of age - there is sufficient to charge. This again is incorrect because of the 'reasonable belief' requirement & due to the 'age' requirements of Armitage for a s.9 offence - although there is a similar s.13 offence where defendants are under 18 - but again the 'reasonable belief' requirement is needed.

Sexual Offences
Child Sex Offences

Question CR/PS/36

Lowden switches on his home computer and finds that he has a number of internet-delivered e-mails waiting to be opened. One such e-mail is untitled and, when he opens it, Lowden finds that it contains obscene pictures of children performing sexual acts. He immediately deletes the e-mail.

Which of the following statements is true in relation to Lowden's criminal liability for making indecent photographs of children under the Protection of Children Act 1978, s.1?

A Lowden will not commit the offence if the e-mail was unsolicited.

B Lowden will not commit the offence if he was unaware that the e-mail contained or was likely to contain indecent images.

C Lowden will commit the offence as soon as he opens the e-mail.

D Lowden will not commit the offence as the image was only on the screen momentarily.

Answer CR/PS/36

B is correct.

Merely opening an untitled e-mail without any reason to believe it contained/was likely to contain an indecent image is not 'making' a photo/pseudo photo - ***R v Smith and Jayson* [2002] EWCA Crim 683** and s.1(a) is not an absolute offence. If Lowden had the relevant knowledge he would commit the offence at the time of opening the e-mail. The time for which the image is on the screen is irrelevant - the offence is concerned with retrieval which is complete here (if Lowden was aware).

Question CR/PS/37

Gargrave is the subject of an application for an Anti-Social Behaviour Order (ASBO) in her local magistrates court. Gargrave's brother, Mansun, believes that one of Gargrave's neighbours is going to provide a witness statement in the ASBO proceedings which started this morning. In an attempt to intimidate the neighbour and stop him giving the statement, Mansun follows him home and threatens to smash up his car if he goes ahead and gives the statement. The neighbour reports the incident to your police station.

In relation to an offence of intimidating witnesses under the Criminal Justice and Police Act 2001, s.39, which of the following is true?

A   Gargrave has committed an arrestable offence.

B   The intimidation has to be committed against a person and, as the threat is made towards property, the offence does not apply here.

C   The offence applies to civil proceedings, including applications for an ASBO.

D   The offence can only be committed in respect of criminal proceedings or other trials and therefore does not apply here.

Answer CR/PS/37

C is correct.

The offence applies to 'relevant proceedings' which includes proceedings in a magistrates' court which are not proceedings for an offence (s.41). The offence does include threats to property and Gargrave is the subject of the ASBO not the person making the threat (i.e. Mansun who would commit the s.39 offence).

Note
Section 110 SOCAP removed the terms 'Arrestable' and 'Serious Arrestable' offences.

Question CR/PS/38

While on supervisory patrol duties you receive a call from a local MP that several foreign nationals are believed to be hiding on a housing estate in her constituency. Enquiries reveal that, although the people concerned were originally granted limited leave to enter the UK, they have overstayed by several months.

In relation to the offence of illegal entry and overstaying (under the Immigration Act 1971, s.24), what specific power of arrest (via s.28A), if any, is available?

A   It is an indictable offence.

B   It is an arrestable offence by virtue of statutory designation under the act.

C   A constable in uniform may arrest without warrant anyone whom he/she has reasonable grounds to suspect of committing the offence.

D   A constable may arrest without warrant anyone whom he/she has reasonable grounds to suspect has committed the offence.

Answer CR/PS/38

D is correct.

This is the statutory power of arrest provision in s. 28A.

s. 28A Immigration Act 1971 states:

> *(i) A constable or immigration officer may arrest without warrant a person -*
> *(a) who has committed or attempted to commit an offence under section 24 or 24A...*

Note
Section 110 SOCAP removed the terms 'Arrestable' and 'Serious Arrestable' offences.

INSPECTORS
Crime

Question CR/I/1

Following an argument Haydon drives her car at her partner, Willis. Willis sustains some internal injuries which are not serious but which require a blood transfusion. Willis, being a Jehovah's Witness refuses the transfusion and eventually dies from his injuries.

For the purposes of 'causation', is Willis' refusal of the transfusion a 'new intervening act'?

A   No, because any peculiar characteristic of a victim will not amount to a new intervening act.

B   Yes, because Willis exercised his own free will in refusing the transfusion.

C   No, because Haydon knew that Willis was a Jehovah's Witness and should have taken this into account when causing his injuries.

D   Yes, because the blood transfusion was proper medical treatment.

Answer CR/I/1

A is correct.

Any peculiar characteristic of a victim will not amount to a new intervening act. Willis' actions are not an exercise of his free will; they are a peculiar characteristic which will not be taken into account when assessing Haydon's liability. Haydon's specific knowledge is not relevant to this aspect of causation (although it may be admitted in evidence to prove the required mens rea or state of mind). Proper medical treatment does not amount to a new intervening act.

Question CR/I/2

Placzek is told by a friend that a form of ecstasy (a controlled drug) can be manufactured by mixing paracetamol with bicarbonate of soda and subjecting the mixture to a heating process. Believing this to be possible, Placzek makes a mixture of the two substances and puts them in a microwave oven.

Has Placzek committed an offence of attempting to produce a controlled drug contrary to the Criminal Attempts Act 1981, section 1?

A   Yes, because he did all he could to bring about the desired consequence, that is, the production of a controlled drug.

B   No, because production of the drug was physically impossible.

C   Yes, because his efforts to produce the drug were more than merely preparatory and he believed that production of the drug was possible.

D   No, because his efforts to produce the drug were merely preparatory.

Answer CR/I/2

C is correct.

Under **s. 1(1) of the Criminal Attempts Act 1981** the person must carry out acts which are more than merely preparatory in order to be guilty of an 'attempt', while **s. 1(2)** provides that, in relation to an 'impossible' offence, the person's conduct will be assessed on the facts 'as they believed them to be'. The offence is about intention as well as 'effort' and physical impossibility is covered by **s. 1(2)**; it is only legal impossibility which is precluded from the Act.

Question CR/I/3

Michaelson is a postman. He is approached on his rounds by two men who threaten him, saying that he must divert a parcel from a sorting office so that they can steal the contents. The men tell Michaelson that if he does not do as they say, they will tell his employer about a previously undisclosed conviction for theft. Michaelson, a very timid person anyway, agrees to do as they say and delivers the parcel to them. Michaelson is later arrested for his part in the offence of theft and demands to talk to an inspector at the police station.

In relation to the defence of duress, which of the following statements is true?

A   The defence will only be available if Michaelson can show that the threat drove him to commit the offence.

B   The defence will not be available as it only applies to offences of murder/attempted murder.

C   The defence will only be available if Michaelson can show that a person of reasonable firmness, would have behaved as he did.

D   The defence will not be available as Michaelson has not been threatened with death or serious injury.

Answer CR/I/3

D is correct.

The defence of duress only applies where the person is threatened with death or serious injury. Had there been such a threat, there would be a need to show that the threat drove him to commit the offence. The defence, if available, does not apply to offences of murder/attempted murder and, if available, requires the defendant to show that a reasonable person sharing the defendant's characteristics would have behaved as the defendant did.

Question CR/I/4

In order to prove the offence of murder it is necessary to show 'malice aforethought'. This means that the defendant:

A   Planned to kill the victim.

B   Was reckless as to whether the victim was killed or not.

C   Intended to kill the victim or to cause them grievous bodily harm.

D   Intended to kill the victim or foresaw that the victim was likely to be killed.

Answer CR/I/4

C is correct.

The courts have held that only an intention to kill or to cause grievous bodily harm will suffice.

Pre-meditation is not required - though it may be evidence to support the relevant intention for the defence of diminished responsibility.

Question CR/I/5

Which of the following is NOT a 'special defence' to the offence of murder?

A   Voluntary intoxication.

B   Provocation.

C   Diminished responsibility.

D   Suicide pact.

Answer CR/I/5

A is correct.

Voluntary intoxication, although a general defence to crimes of specific intent, is not one of the 'special defences' which can be used for the offence of murder.

Question CR/I/6

A doctor agrees to a request by her terminally-ill patient to help him take his own life. Being fully aware of the consequences, she provides her patient with a very large dose of medication. The patient dies as a result of the overdose.

What is the doctor's criminal liability in relation to the death of the patient?

A   She commits the offence of murder, although she has a possible defence of provocation.

B   She commits the offence of manslaughter because she assisted the patient in pursuance of a suicide pact.

C   She commits the offence of murder.

D   She commits the offence of manslaughter by an unlawful act.

Answer CR/I/6

C is correct.

All the ingredients of murder are present. Provocation does not apply - there has been no sudden 'loss of control'. A suicide pact must envisage the ultimate death of all the people involved.

Question CR/I/7

Bryant finds a syringe containing a controlled drug on some waste ground. Bryant suspects that the syringe contains a controlled drug. As he has an appointment at the doctors' surgery the following week, Bryant puts the syringe in his pocket and, several days later, takes it with him to his general practitioner. He hands it to the doctor who immediately destroys it.

Who, if either, has a specific defence to an offence of possessing a controlled drug under the Misuse of Drugs Act 1971?

A   The doctor.

B   Bryant.

C   Both Bryant and the doctor.

D   Neither Bryant nor the doctor.

Answer CR/I/7

A is correct.

The doctor is a person lawfully entitled to possess the drug under these circumstances. Bryant does not take all such steps as are reasonably open to him to destroy/deliver the drug as soon as possible after finding it.

Question CR/I/8

Russell is a chemist working for a pharmaceutical company. She uses the laboratory facilities of her employer to create various 'designer' drugs which she sells to her friends. One evening Russell is experimenting with some diamorphine (a Class A controlled drug) which she converts to a type of heroin (also a Class A controlled drug).

Does Russell commit an offence of producing a controlled drug under section 4 of the Misuse of Drugs Act 1971?

A   No, because she has not 'produced' anything new by converting an existing controlled drug.

B   Yes, because she is in unlawful possession of the first controlled drug.

C   No, because she is a person lawfully entitled to possess or produce controlled drugs under the Misuse of Drugs Regulations.

D   Yes, because conversion of a controlled drug of one Class to a controlled drug of another Class amounts to 'production'.

Answer CR/I/8

D is correct.

Conversion of a controlled drug of one Class to a controlled drug of another Class amounts to 'production'. She has 'produced' another drug and possession is irrelevant here. She is not acting within the scope of her employment.

Question CR/I/9

You are the inspector in charge of a small specialist unit set up to deal with the rising cases of supplying child pornography. One of your officers has been assigned to undercover duties where he is posing as a photographer and frequenting clubs and functions known to be used by those engaged in the sale and supply of child pornography. The officer is approached by Armstrong who believes the officer supplies child pornography and asks him to supply whatever pornographic pictures of children he can for a group of men in the town. The undercover officer seeks your advice on what action, if any, can be taken against Armstrong.

In relation to the advice you would give the officer which one of the following statements is correct?

A   Armstrong cannot be charged with any offence as the officer had no intention of supplying the pornography.

B   Armstrong may be charged with incitement but only where another member of the 'group of men' can be implicated as this offence requires the intention of at least two parties.

C   Armstrong cannot be charged with any offence as it is both unfair and an abuse of process if a person is incited by an undercover officer.

D   Armstrong may be charged with incitement as the intent of the person incited is irrelevant.

Answer CR/I/9

D is correct.

In common law it is an offence unlawfully to incite another to commit an offence.

In *R v Loosley*; **Attorney-General's Reference (No. 3) of 2000 [2001] 1 WLR 2060**, the House of Lords held that although it is both unfair and an abuse of process if a person is incited by an undercover officer to commit an offence where the officer only offered the person an 'unexceptional opportunity' to commit an offence, this would not amount to an abuse of process.

In *DPP v Armstrong* **[2000] Crim LR 379** it was held that the intent of the person incited was irrelevant, that is the undercover officer had no intention of supplying pornography.

Question CR/I/10

You are the inspector in charge of an Administration of Justice department and your advice is sought about the following case. After the execution of a search warrant at the home of Adams a small quantity of controlled drugs have been found. The drugs were not owned by Adams and she alleged she was unaware they were in her home. However, she did admit that persons visiting her home were highly likely to have brought controlled drugs with them but on no occasion did she personally use the drugs or have physical possession of them.

In these circumstances would you advise that Adams be charged with an offence of possessing the controlled drugs?

A   No, Adams did not have or know that she had controlled drugs in her actual possession even though they were found in her home.

B   Yes, Adams was aware that others were bringing controlled drugs into her home with the intention of taking them and it could be inferred she had control over the drugs.

C   No, Adams did not have possession of a controlled drug unless she explicitly gave consent for the use of controlled drugs in her home.

D   Yes, Adams had given implied consent to others to use controlled drugs in her home and this would constitute possession.

Answer CR/I/10

A is correct.

In *Adams v DPP* **[2002] EWHC 438** it was held that where the owner of a house knew that visitors were in possession of controlled drugs and intending to use them this was not sufficient evidence to infer that the owner had control over the drugs. Even giving explicit or implied consent for the use of a controlled drug did not itself constitute possession by the owner. Possession of a controlled drug can only be proved where a person had a controlled drug actually in their physical possession and knew that it was a controlled drug.

Question CR/I/11

Ireland, a 30 year old woman, learns about an extra-marital affair which her husband has been having with his accountant. Ireland begins to make frequent telephone calls to the accountant, remaining silent when the accountant answers. After several months the accountant begins to suffer considerable anxiety and stress for which she receives psychiatric treatment.

Has Ireland committed an 'assault' on the accountant?

A   No, because she was not 'present' with the accountant at the time of the telephone calls, therefore the threats were not 'immediate'.

B   No, because mere silence is an omission rather than an act.

C   Yes, because the persistent telephone calls followed by silences can amount to an application of unlawful force.

D   Yes, because she intended the accountant to fear the application of unlawful force in the immediate future.

Answer CR/I/11

C is correct.

The persistent telephone calls followed by silences have been held to be capable of amounting to an application of unlawful force (*R v Ireland* **[1998] AC 147).**

There is no requirement for a physical presence at the time of the assault.

The defendant here actually applied unlawful force rather than simply creating a fear of such an application in the future.

Question CR/I/12

Ingleton is in the high street when he hears a police officer asking someone some questions about an accident which they had witnessed earlier that day. In order to make it as difficult as possible for the officer to do her job, Ingleton stands between the officer and the witness and pretends to start a conversation with him. Despite requests from the officer for Ingleton to go away, he continues to interrupt the witness. Ingleton begins to contradict the witness' answers, pretending that he was there when the accident happened. Although the witness finds the whole episode amusing, Ingleton eventually makes it impossible for the officer to speak to the witness and she arrests Ingleton for obstructing her in the execution of her duty (under the **Police Act 1996, section 89**).

Was the officer's arrest lawful under s.89?

A   No, there has been no physical obstruction in these circumstances.

B   Yes, there has been sufficient obstruction for the purposes of the Act.

C   No, there is no obligation on the witness to answer any questions and therefore the officer is not acting in 'the execution of her duty'.

D   No, there is no power of arrest for the offence unless it is accompanied by a breach/threatened breach of the peace.

Answer CR/I/12

D is correct.

There is no power of arrest for the offence unless it is accompanied by a breach/threatened breach of the peace. There does not need to be a physical obstruction for this offence. Although there is no obligation on the witness to answer any of these questions, it is still a legitimate part of the officer's duty to ask such questions.

Question CR/I/13

Following a disturbance in a pub, Karadicz is arrested in order to prevent a breach of the peace. His friend, Jefferies, feels aggrieved by the arrest and tells the arresting officer that Karadicz has done nothing wrong. When the officer takes no notice of him, Jefferies tries to free his friend, and pushes the officer. She trips, causing a deep gash down to the bone in her cheek and breaks her hip. Jefferies says that he did not intend to injure the officer but simply wanted to set his friend free. It is later decided by a court that the arrest of Karadicz was unlawful as there had been no lawful reason to apprehend for a renewed breach of the peace at the time of the arrest.

On these facts, does Jefferies still commit an offence under s.18 of the Offences Against the Person Act 1861?

A   No, because the arrest which he sought to prevent was unlawful and he did not intend to injure the officer.

B   No, because he did not 'wound' the officer or 'inflict' grievous bodily harm.

C   Yes, because he intended to resist the arrest of Karadicz.

D   Yes, because he should have foreseen the likelihood of some injury, albeit it slight, to the officer.

Answer CR/I/13

A is correct.

There must be an intention to resist or prevent the lawful apprehension or detainer (arrest) of another, or to do some grievous bodily harm. He did 'wound' the officer and caused her grievous bodily harm, but the arrest was unlawful. This offence is one which requires 'specific intent', not simply objective foresight.

Question CR/I/14

When driving home from work, an off-duty police officer becomes involved in an argument with a fellow motorist at the roadside. The other motorist swears at the off-duty officer and makes insulting remarks about her appearance. Enraged by this abuse, the off-duty officer grabs a CS gas canister from her car and sprays it at the motorist. The spray misses the motorist who jumps into his car and drives away unhurt.

Which of the following statements is correct in relation to the officer's liability for 'administering a noxious substance' under s. 23 of the Offences Against the Person Act 1861?

A   She commits the offence because she has acted 'unlawfully and maliciously in administering a 'noxious thing'.

B   She does not commit any offence because the CS spray is not a 'destructive or noxious thing' for the purpose of the Act.

C   She does not commit the offence because she has not caused the other motorist grievous bodily harm or endangered his life.

D   She commits the offence because she intended to cause the motorist grievous bodily harm or to endanger his life.

Answer CR/I/14

C is correct.

The offence under **s. 23 Offences Against the Person Act 1861** is one of consequence, that is, you must show that the defendant's behaviour either endangered the person's life or that it brought about grievous bodily harm. Although the officer does appear to have acted unlawfully and maliciously, the requirements as to the consequences of her actions have not been met. Her intention is not relevant to this offence **(it is relevant to the s. 24 offence)**.

Question CR/I/15

What is the required 'state of mind' for the offences of false imprisonment and kidnapping?

A   'Specific intent'.

B   Objective recklessness.

C   Subjective recklessness.

D   Strict liability.

Answer CR/I/15

C is correct.

Only subjective recklessness (i.e. proof that the defendant was aware that there was some risk involved in his or her conduct but that they nevertheless went ahead with their conduct). 'Specific intent' is too high a level of mens rea for this offence while the other options are too low a level of mens rea for this offence.

Question CR/I/16

Following a night out with his wife, Fotheringham returns to his home where Davies, his 24 year old nephew is babysitting for the Fotheringham's children. After Mrs Fotheringham has gone to bed, Fotheringham, who is very drunk, sits up talking to Davies and mistakenly believes that Davies is 'making a pass' at him. Fotheringham begins to fondle Davies who does not want anything to do with his uncle but is too frightened to say anything. Fotheringham is too drunk to consider whether or not Davies is consenting and tries to have anal sex with him, but only achieves partial penetration before giving up and falling asleep. The following day Davies reports that he has been 'raped'.

In relation to the allegation (s.1 Sexual Offences Act 2003), which of the following statements is true?

A   The offence of rape does not extend to anal sex therefore the allegation is wrong.

B   The required 'criminal conduct' is penetration to any degree, therefore that part of the offence is complete.

C   s.75 Evidential Presumption and Consent places a requirement on the defence to prove the required 'state of mind' or belief that Davies does not consent.

D   The offence of rape requires an act of sexual intercourse without the victim's consent. As no sexual intercourse has taken place, the appropriate charge is 'attempted rape'.

Answer CR/I/16

B is correct.

Partial penetration will suffice for the offence of rape. **Section 75 (Sexual Offences Act 2003) - Evidential Presumptions and Consent** places the requirement on the prosecution to show that the defendant carried out the relevant act and **not the DEFENCE**. If a defendant knows that the other person might not consent or if the defendant is too drunk to consider whether the person is consenting, this will suffice. The offence of rape does extend to anal sex.

Question CR/I/17

In order to 'help' some of her women friends earn some money, Gill voluntarily takes phone calls from mobile phone customers who later pay to have sexual intercourse with those friends. Although she gets no personal benefit or reward, Gill spends several hours a day arranging for the women to be in particular places at the agreed times, manages their earnings and organises their days off.

On the given facts, does Gill commit an offence of causing, inciting or controlling prostitution under s.53 of the Sexual Offences Act 2003?

A   No, because her activities are solely concerned with the administration of their existing activities.

B   No, because the offence can only be committed by a man.

C   Yes, because all the ingredients of the offence are present.

D   No, because she does not receive any personal gain by doing so.

Answer CR/I/17

D is correct.

The offence requires the person to carry out the prohibited behaviour for the purpose of gain.

The offence can be committed by a man or a woman.

The Sexual Offences Act 2003, s.53 states:

(1) A person commits an offence if -
  (a) he intentionally controls any of the activities of another person relating to that person's prostitution in any part of the world, and
  (b) he does so for or in the expectation of gain for himself or a third person.

Question CR/I/18

'Family Members' are defined under Sexual Offences Act 2003, ss. 25-26.

Which of the following sexual relationships fall outside the definition of a 'family member'?

A   Grandfather with grand-daughter.

B   Brother with half-sister.

C   Two divorcees each have a child of 17 who are engaged in a sexual relationship before their respective parent marries and move all four of them into the same household.

D   Sister with half-brother born outside wedlock.

Answer CR/I/18

C is correct.

'Family Members' are defined under Sexual Offences Act 2003, ss. 25-26.

Two divorcees who each have a child of 17 who are engaged in a sexual relationship **BEFORE** their respective parent marries and move all four of them into the same household is the only relationship which is exempted from ss. 25-26.

Question CR/I/19

Mansun is a hotel porter. He has a sexual fetish which involves gaining sexual gratification from touching womens gloves. One morning Mansun offers to carry the handbag and gloves of a female guest who is carrying the items in the hotel lobby. The woman refuses his offer but, as she climbs the stairs in front of him, Mansun shouts "give me that" in a menacing tone. He grabs one of the gloves from the woman who, being frightened, lets go of it. Mansun caresses the glove for several seconds before throwing it on the floor and running off. When questioned, Mansun admits that he was motivated by sexual desire in pulling the glove from the woman.

The Investigating Officer wants the custody officer to charge Mansun with 'sexual assault'.

Under these circumstances, has Mansun committed an offence of Sexual Assault by Touching under s.3 Sexual Offences Act 2003?

A   Yes, a sexual assault is simply an assault accompanied by 'sexual' circumstances of indecency which is what has happened in this case.

B   No, the act of removing the glove is not 'sexual' (as per. s.78 of the act) in itself and Mansun's secret intentions can not make it so.

C   No, the only force which was used in this case was applied to the glove, therefore there has been no assault.

D   No, the woman was unaware of Mansun's 'sexual' intentions.

Answer CR/I/19

B is correct.

Section 78 of the Sexual Offences Act 2003 provides that penetration, touching or any other activity will be sexual if a reasonable person would consider that:

(a) whatever its circumstances or any person's purpose in relation to it, it is sexual by its very nature or,

(b) because of its nature it may be sexual and because of its circumstances or the purpose of any person in relation to it, it is sexual.

If the activity would not appear to a reasonable person to be sexual, then it will not meet either criteria and, irrespective of any sexual gratification the person might derive from it will not make the act 'sexual'. Thus a secretly harboured 'fetish' cannot make an otherwise innocuous act 'sexual' - thus no offence is committed.

Question CR/I/20

At a party in a Students' Union bar, Bridget slips a hefty dose of her mother's Valium, a sedative, into her friend Ella's cider so that William, a fellow student can help Ella home and have sexual intercourse with her while she is unconscious. Ella drinks the cider and becomes very drowsy. William helps Ella back to her house and removes her clothes, sexually assaulting her but not attempting sexual intercourse.

Does Bridget commit the offence of Administering a Substance with Intent under s. 61 of the Sexual Offences Act 2003?

A   Yes, because Bridget's intention at the time of giving Ella the drug was to enable William to have unlawful sexual intercourse with her.

B   No, because the offence can only be committed by a man.

C   No, because unlawful sexual intercourse did not take place.

D   Yes, because the offence includes an intention to enable any man to sexually assault the woman while she is stupefied.

Answer CR/I/20

A is correct.

The Sexual Offences Act 2003, s.61 states:

(1) A person commits an offence if he intentionally administers a substance to, or causes a substance to be taken by, another person (B)-
   (a) knowing that B does not consent, and
   (b) with the intention of stupefying or overpowering B, so as to enable any person to engage in a sexual activity that involves B.

Thus the offence is one of specific intent and that intent was present at the time Bridget caused Ella to take the drug. There is no requirement for unlawful sexual intercourse to take place. The offence can be committed by a man or a woman.

Question CR/I/21

Which of the following people would NOT be 'a person connected with a child' for the purposes of an offence under s. 1 of the Child Abduction Act 1984?

A   A person who is reasonably believed to be the child's father, but who is not lawfully married to the child's mother.

B   The child's guardian.

C   The child's aunt who has custody of the child.

D   The child's 18 year old brother living with the child.

Answer CR/I/21

D is correct.

The brother, even though he is connected genetically with the child, does not come within the categories of person outlined under **s. 1 of the Child Abduction Act 1984**.

Question CR/I/22

In relation to an offence of child cruelty under s.1 of the Children and Young Persons Act 1933, which of the following statements is true?

A The victim must be under 15 years old.

B The person committing the offence must have attained the age of 17 years.

C The victim must be under the age of 16 years old.

D The person committing the offence must have attained the age of 15 years.

Answer CR/I/22

C is correct.

The section specifies that the offence can only be committed in relation to a person under the age of 16 years.

Question CR/I/23

During a search, Bahatti is found to have indecent photographs of children in his house. Bahatti admits that the photographs are his and that he took them himself. He stresses however, that the photographs were for his own purposes and were not intended to be shown to anyone else.

Assuming that he did not intend to show the photographs to anyone else which, if any, of the following offences may Bahatti be charged with?

A   An offence under s. 1 of the Protection of Children Act 1978 only.

B   An offence under s. 160 of the Criminal Justice Act 1988 only.

C   Both.

D   Neither.

Answer CR/I/23

C is correct.

He commits an offence under **s. 1 of the Protection of Children Act 1978** by taking the photographs and under **s. 160 of the Criminal Justice Act 1988** by possessing them. He commits an offence by simple possession under the **Criminal Justice Act 1988**. Although he does not intend to show or distribute the photographs, Bahatti commits an offence when he takes them.

Question CR/I/24

Where a child has been taken into police protection under s.46 of the Children Act 1989, what is the maximum length of time that the child can be so kept?

A   48 hours.

B   24 hours.

C   36 hours.

D   72 hours.

Answer CR/I/24

D is correct.

72 hours is the limit set out at **s.46(6) of the Children Act 1989**.

Question CR/I/25

Following an examination by a doctor, a child has been detained by a constable at a hospital under the provisions of **s. 46 of the Children Act 1989**. The child's 18 year old brother learns that the child is being kept there and comes to the hospital. Although he is told that the child is being detained under **section 46**, the brother entices the child to sneak out of an examination room window and they both return home.

What specific power of arrest (under s.49), if any, is provided for your officers in this situation?

A   It is an arrestable offence.

B   There is no specific power of arrest for this offence. Your officers should consider using their powers under s.24 PACE [as introduced by s.110] provided the circumstances meet the 'necessity' test.

C   The Act provides a constable with a power to arrest, without warrant, any person reasonably suspected of having committed an offence under s. 46.

D   The Act provides a constable with a power to arrest, without warrant, any person reasonably suspected of having committed, or of being about to commit, an offence under s. 46.

Answer CR/I/25

B is correct.
There is no specific power of arrest under available under **s.49 of the Children Act 1989**.

The offence is not listed as an arrestable offence in the **Police & Criminal Evidence Act 1984** and it only carries a maximum of 6 months' imprisonment. However, the general arrest condition under **s.25(3)(e) of PACE** would probably apply. As a result of the introduction of **Section 110 of the Serious Orgainsed Crime and Police Act (SOCAP) s.24 of PACE** has been altered. In essence there is no longer a legal concept of 'Arrestable' and 'Serious Arrestable' offences. A constable now has a power of arrest for all offences subject to the 'necessity' test.

Question CR/I/26

The longest a person may be kept at a 'place of safety' under the provisions of the Mental Health Act 1983 (s.136) is:-

A   48 hours.

B   24 hours.

C   36 hours.

D   72 hours.

Answer CR/I/26

D is correct.

72 hours is the limit set out in **s.136(2) of the Mental Health Act 1983.**

Question CR/I/27

Reece is appointed as a trustee to hold property for the benefit of a small group of people originally formed by his grandfather to carry out charitable works abroad. After 20 years all of the organisation's original members have died or moved abroad themselves. Reece, having taken all reasonable steps to discover their whereabouts, sells the property and gives the proceeds, which run to several thousand pounds, to a local church fund.

For the purposes of the Theft Act 1968, what effect do the exceptions under s. 2(1)(c) have in deciding whether Reece's actions were dishonest?

A   His actions will not be regarded as dishonest because he took all reasonable steps to discover the people to whom the property belonged.

B   His actions will not be regarded as dishonest because he believed that the people to whom the property belonged could not be discovered by taking all reasonable steps.

C   His actions may still be regarded as dishonest because he came by the property as a trustee.

D   His actions may still be regarded as dishonest because he parted with the property under conditions which made it an outright appropriation.

Answer CR/I/27

C is correct.

The exception to 'dishonesty' under s. 2(1)(c) does not apply where the person has come by the property as a trustee. The conditions of the parting with the property are not relevant to the issue of dishonesty under s. 2(1)(c).

Question CR/I/28

Hussein, a heavy smoker, is travelling on a train to London for a meeting. Finding himself out of cigarettes, Hussein walks down the carriage and sees a carton of 200 cigarettes on another passenger's table. The other passenger is not there so Hussein takes a pack of 20 cigarettes from the carton. He leaves a Post-It Note on top of the carton, addressed to the other passenger, advising them that he has 'borrowed' a packet of cigarettes and will pay £5 for them. On the Post-It Note Hussein leaves his name, address, e-mail address and details of the carriage where he can be found. On returning to his seat, the other passenger finds the Post-It Note and summons the guard, reporting the 'theft' of 20 cigarettes.

How do the provisions of section 2(2) of the Theft Act 1968 affect Hussein's criminal liability in these circumstances?

A   Hussein's actions may be dishonest irrespective of his willingness to pay for the cigarettes.

B   Hussein's actions will not be regarded as dishonest, provided he can show that his willingness to pay for the cigarettes was genuine and honestly held.

C   Hussein's actions will not be regarded as dishonest as he has taken all reasonable steps to pay for the cigarettes.

D   Hussein's actions may be dishonest notwithstanding his willingness to pay for the cigarettes but his leaving of personal details in order to make restitution will, of itself, negate any dishonesty.

Answer CR/I/28

A is correct.

Section 2(1)(c) of the Theft Act 1968 provides that a person's appropriation of property may be dishonest notwithstanding that (s)he is willing to pay for it.

The fact that the genuineness or otherwise of his willingness to pay is irrelevant for the purposes of s. 2(2), as is the taking of reasonable steps irrelevant for the purposes of s. 2(2). The leaving of his personal details will not, of itself, negate any dishonesty **(Boggelin v Williams [1978] 1 WLR 873)**.

Question CR/I/29

Two youths go into a corner shop and, for a practical joke, switch the price labels around on the items displayed on the shelves making some items appear to be more expensive than they should be and others less so. Having switched the labels, the youths run off without the shopkeeper realising what they have done.

Under s. 3 of the Theft Act 1968, have the youths 'appropriated' the items by switching the labels round?

A   No, because they have not acted 'dishonestly'.

B   No, because they have no intent of permanently depriving the owner of the items.

C   No, because their behaviour has not amounted to an outright taking of the items.

D   Yes, because they have assumed the rights of owner.

Answer CR/I/29

D is correct.

They have assumed the right of the shopkeeper to affix price labels on his/her goods. In light of the decision in *R v Gomez* **[1993] AC 442**, this means that they have appropriated the items. The issue of 'dishonesty' is a separate one that needs to be determined independently of the issue of appropriation. There is no requirement for there to have been an outright taking.

Question CR/I/30

In relation to s. 3 of the Theft Act 1968, which of the following statements is correct?

A   An assumption of any of the owner's rights, if made with his/her consent, will not be an 'appropriation'.

B   An element of dishonesty is necessary before there can be an 'appropriation'.

C   An assumption of a right of ownership after coming by property innocently can not be an 'appropriation'.

D   An 'appropriation' can be a continuous act and does not suddenly cease.

Answer CR/I/30

D is correct.

The decisions in *R v Hale* **(1978) 68 Cr App R 415** and *R v Gomez* **[1993] AC 442** make it clear that an 'appropriation' can be a continuing act. There can be an appropriation even though the owner consents. The issue of dishonesty is separate from that of 'appropriation' - although s. 3(2) blurs the distinction slightly by referring to someone acting in good faith.

Question CR/I/31

Police officers are called to a council estate where officials from the local authority are repossessing one of their houses. The officials tell the police officers that there are several items that are missing from the house, including a fireplace and a row of kitchen units both of which were let to be used with the house. The officials believe that the tenant, Musgrove, has sold the fireplace and the kitchen units and say that they want to bring charges against her for theft.

Under these circumstances, what is the legal status of the fireplace and the kitchen units?

A   They are property that can be 'stolen' for the purposes of the Theft Act 1968 but not damaged for the purposes of the Criminal Damage Act 1971.

B   They are property that can be both 'stolen' for the purposes of the Theft Act 1968, and 'damaged' for the purposes of the criminal Damage Act 1971.

C   They are part of the 'land' and therefore not property that can be 'stolen' for the purposes of the Theft Act 1968, even though they are property for the purposes of the Criminal Damage Act 1971.

D   They are part of the 'land' and therefore not property that can be either 'stolen' for the purposes of the Theft Act 1968, or damaged for the purposes of the Criminal Damage Act 1971.

Answer CR/I/31

B is correct.

Section 4(2)(c) of the Theft Act 1968 says that fixtures or structures let to be used with land that are appropriated by someone under a tenancy can be 'stolen'. Because **s.10 of the Criminal Damage Act 1971** includes property of a tangible nature, whether real or personal, they can also be damaged.

Question CR/I/32

Hale, a shoplifter, is disturbed while taking some clothes from a rack by a store detective. Although he had decided to steal the clothes before taking them from the rack, Hale abandons them and tries to escape through the fire exit. As he runs out, Hale threatens a shop assistant, telling her to get out of the way or he'll stab her.

Has Hale committed robbery under s.8 of the Theft Act 1968?

A No, he has not 'used force on any person' and so he does not commit the offence.

B No, he has not stolen anything and so he does not commit the offence.

C Yes, he has both stolen property (the clothes) and has used force on another person therefore he commits the offence.

D No, he has not used force 'in order to steal' so he does not commit the offence.

Answer CR/I/32

D is correct.

The theft is complete and Hale's use of force is solely related to his escape. If he had kept the clothes and tried to get them out of the shop with him, it might be argued that the theft was still 'in progress' at the time the force was used. He did threaten force, which is covered by s.8 and stole the clothes by taking them from the rack with the requisite intent (*R v Gomez* **[1993] AC 442**), but he did not use/threaten force in order to steal.

Question CR/I/33

In relation to an offence of supplying a controlled drug contrary to s. 4(3) of the Misuse of Drugs Act 1971 which one of the following sets of circumstances has been held NOT to amount to supplying?

A A Rastafarian supplying others as part of their religious worship.

B An intention to return the drugs to their depositor.

C Assisting in pushing down the plunger of a syringe that another person was already using.

D A police informer providing a controlled drug to another in order that the other be arrested.

Answer CR/I/33

C is correct.

In *R v Harris* **[1968] 1 WLR 769** it was held that assisting in the pushing down the plunger of a syringe did not amount to 'supplying'.

The other three answers have been held to by 'supplying': a Rastafarian supplying others as part of their religious worship (*R v Taylor* **[2002] 1 Cr App R 314**); an intention to return the drugs to their depositor (*R v Panton* **(2001)** *The Times*, **27 March**); a police informer providing a controlled drug to another in order that the other be arrested (*R v X* **[1994] Crim LR 827**).

Question CR/I/34

The **Criminal Justice and Police Act 2001** makes provision for courts to impose travel restrictions on offenders convicted of drug trafficking offences.

In relation to travel restriction orders which one of the following statements is correct?

A   Where an offender is sentenced to four years imprisonment or more an order may be made lasting for a minimum of two years and the offender may be required to surrender their passport.

B   Where an offender is sentenced to two years imprisonment or more an order may be made lasting for a minimum of one year and the offender may be required to surrender their passport.

C   Where an offender is sentenced to four years imprisonment or more an order may be made lasting for a minimum of one year and the offender must be required to surrender their passport.

D   Where an offender is sentenced to two years imprisonment or more an order may be made lasting for a minimum of two years and the offender must be required to surrender their passport.

Answer CR/I/34

A is correct.

The Criminal Justice and Police Act 2001 s. 33 provides that where a court has convicted a person of a drug trafficking offence and it has determined that a sentence of four years or more is appropriate it is under a duty to consider whether or not a travel restriction order would be appropriate. Such an order is for a minimum period of two years and an offender may also be required to surrender their passport as part of the order.

Question CR/I/35

You are investigating an internal complaint against a police officer using a force computer. On inspecting the relevant computer you find a number of indecent images of children on the internet 'cache directory' on the hard drive. These images have been downloaded from the Internet.

In relation to an offence of 'making' images of children (under the Protection of Children Act 1978, s.1), which of the following statements is true?

A Downloading the images will amount to 'making' them.

B Downloading the images will not amount to 'making' them.

C The amount of time the images were on the computer screen is relevant for the purposes of proving the offence.

D Creating pseudo-images of children is not included in the expression 'making'.

Answer CR/I/35

A is correct.

Merely downloading an image will suffice *R v Bowden* **[2000] 2 WLR 1083**. Pseudo-photographs are covered and, once downloaded, the amount of time the image is on the screen is irrelevant – *R v Smith and Jayson* **[2002] EWCA Crim 683**.

Question CR/I/36

Acting on information received, police officers stop a heavy goods vehicle which has entered the United Kingdom via a port in the South East of England. On searching the vehicle, which is owned by a haulage company, the officers discover several men and women hiding in the back of the trailer unit. The men and women claim to be 'asylum seekers' fleeing from central Europe. The officers want to arrest the driver and detain the vehicle and they seek your advice.

Which of the following correctly describes the relevant police powers in relation to an offence of assisting or harbouring illegal entrants (under the Immigration Act 1971, s.25)?

A   It is an indictable offence but with no specific power to detain the vehicle.

B   It is an indictable offence with a specific power to detain the vehicle.

C   It has a specific power of arrest but with no specific power to detain the vehicle.

D   It has a specific power of arrest with a specific power to detain the vehicle.

Answer CR/I/36

B is correct.

The offence carries 14 years' imprisonment, making it an indictable offence, and there is a power to detain the vehicle in these circumstances under s.25 of the 1971 Act. **Section 110 of the Serious Organised Crime and Police Act 2005** effectively removed the legal terms 'Arrestable' and 'Serious Arrestable' offences.

'Indictable' means triable at Crown Court and includes offences triable either way.

Question CR/I/37

Baldwell is a sex offender and is about to be made the subject of a Sexual Offences Prevention Order (SOPO). You are approached by the DC in the case who tells you that the application is to be made in two weeks' time but Baldwell has tried to intimidate a witness who is to give evidence in support of the SOPO application.

In relation to the offence of witness intimidation (under the Criminal Justice and Police Act 2001, s.39), which of the following statements is correct?

A The offence is not made out as the proceedings have not yet commenced.

B The prosecution must prove Baldwell's intention to pervert, obstruct or interfere with the course of justice and can only do so by direct evidence.

C There is no need to prove any intention to pervert the course of justice as this is a separate offence at common law.

D The prosecution must prove Baldwell's intention to pervert, obstruct or interfere with the course of justice but can do so by irrebuttable presumption based on his conduct.

Answer CR/I/37

A is correct.

An element of the offence is that it is done after the commencement of relevant proceedings **(s.39(1)(c))** - this includes civil proceedings i.e. a SOPO. There is a need to prove the intention to pervert, obstruct or interfere with the course of justice but that can be done by indirect evidence in the form of a rebuttable presumption – not an irrebuttable presumption, and the fact that there is an offence at common law is irrelevant.

Question CR/I/38

You are reviewing a proposed prosecution file in respect of May who is charged with recklessly causing criminal damage to a number of high value cars on a garage forecourt. May, who has learning difficulties, claimed in interview that he had not foreseen the consequences of his actions and that, if he had stopped and thought about them, he would not have behaved as he did.

In relation to the relevant state of mind (mens rea) to support this charge, which of the following statements is true?

A   The risk of damage must have been apparent to May himself.

B   The risk of damage need only have been apparent to a reasonable person even if it had not been obvious to May himself.

C   The risk of damage must have been foreseeable as a 'near certainty' to a reasonable person.

D   The risk of damage is irrelevant here.

Answer CR/I/38

A is correct.

As a result of *R v G and R* **[2003] 3 WLR 1060** 'subjective recklessness' is now used when assessing whether a person acts recklessly for the purposes of *s.1(1) Criminal Damage Act 1971:*

- with respect to a circumstance when he/she is aware of a risk that existed or would exist;
- with respect to a result or consequence when s/he is aware of a risk that it would occur and it is, in the circumstances known to him/her, unreasonable to take the risk.

Note
The ruling for Simple Damage has now changed. The test applied was formerly 'Caldwell recklessness' (per *Metropolitan Police Commissioner v Caldwell* **[1982] AC 341**) which would have meant that the option – the risk of damage need only have been apparent to a reasonable person even if it had not been obvious to May himself - would have been correct.

However the ruling in *R v G and R* **[2003] 3 WLR 1060** is now the 'accepted' standard i.e. 'subjective recklessness' - which makes the option - the risk of damage must have been apparent to May himself - the correct option.

Criminal Damage
Simple Damage

Question CR/I/39

You are the PACE inspector for a police station where Sookoo has been detained. Sookoo has been in police detention for 15 hours under a different name which he gave when arrested. In addition to all the administrative consequences of having the wrong name for the prisoner, officers investigating Sookoo's activities have wasted in excess of 60 hours of police time pursing false leads, along with arresting an innocent member of the public. The custody officer now wants to charge Sookoo with perverting the course of justice at common law.

Can she do so?

A   No, the proper charge is one of 'wasting police time'.

B   No, the course of justice has not been perverted by Sookoo's behaviour.

C   No, the proper charge is one of attempting to pervert the course of justice.

D   Yes, all the ingredients of the offence are present here.

Answer CR/I/39

D is correct.

This is consistent with the decision of the Court of Appeal in *R v Sookoo* (2002) *The Times*, **10 April**. If the attempt to conceal his identity had been crude and unconvincing, with no real consequences for the police or the public, the charge would still have been technically appropriate but should not have been charged in practice (per Sookoo). The existence of the alternative 'wasting police time' offence is irrelevant here.

FREE Trial
MCQ Interactive CD-ROM

MCQ Interactive, the computerised question and answer programme, is easy to use, even for complete computer novices, and it contains the full range of MCQs which can be infinitely regenerated. You can also prepare your own MCQs with MCQ Designer.

To claim your FREE Trial copy of the MCQ Interactive CD-ROM complete this order form below and attach one token from each of the other three MCQ Books on the reverse of this page. You need only complete one order form.

Return the order form (FREEPOST) to:

**Detail Technologies Limited, FREEPOST
PO Box 43, Porth, CF39 8WR.**

Name:	
Rank:	
Address:	
County:	Postcode:
Daytime Telephone No:	
Email Address:	
Mobile Tel. No:	
Mobile Provider:	
Police Force:	

☐ Tick this box if you do not want us to send you information on other related products and offers.

FREE Trial
MCQ Interactive CD-ROM

Attach your three tokens from the other MCQ Books in the spaces provided below. Complete the order form overleaf and return to **Detail Technologies Limited, FREEPOST PO Box 43, Porth, CF39 8WR.**

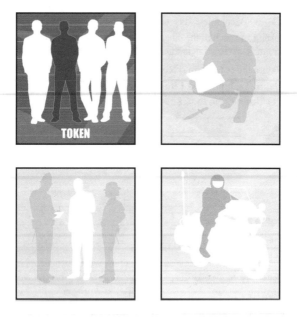